A TRIBUTE TO

Mom

*A heartwarming collection
of stories, quotes and writings
just for Mothers*

ISBN 1-889116-12-2

Printed in the United States of America

First U.S. Edition

Design by
Paragon Communications Group, Inc., Tulsa, Oklahoma

Published by
PENBROOKE PUBLISHING
Tulsa, Oklahoma

A TRIBUTE TO

Mom

PENBROOKE
PUBLISHING

TULSA, OKLAHOMA

Dedicated To:

_____

_____

_____

_____

Only One Mother

*H*undreds of stars in the pretty sky,
Hundreds of shells on the shore together,
Hundreds of birds that go singing by,
Hundreds of birds in the sunny weather.

Hundreds of dewdrops to greet the dawn,
Hundreds of bees in the purple clover,
Hundreds of butterflies on the lawn,
But only one mother the wide world over.

Anonymous

Mother, do you know, almost all people love their mothers, but I have never met anybody in my life, I think, who loved her mother as much as I love you. I don't believe there ever was anybody who did, quite so much, and quite in so many wonderful ways.

Edna St. Vincent Millay to her Mother

When God thought of Mother,
He must have laughed with satisfaction,
and framed it quickly—
so rich, so deep, so divine,
so full of soul, power, and beauty,
was the conception.

Henry Ward Beecher

In the sheltered simplicity of
the first days after a baby is born,
one sees again the magical closed circle,
the miraculous sense of two people
existing only for
each other.

Anne Morrow Lindbergh

To Thee I'll Return

To thee I'll return, overburdened with care;
The heart's dearest solace will smile on me there;
No more from that cottage again will I roam;
Be it ever so humble, there's no place like home.
Home, home, sweet, sweet home!
There's no place like home,
Oh, there's no place like home.

John Howard Payne

*A*mother is someone who dreams
great dreams for you, but then
she lets you chase the dreams
you have for yourself
and loves you
just the same.

Anonymous

Once upon a memory,
Someone wiped away a tear,
Held me close and loved me.
Thank you, Mother dear.

She is just an extraordinary mother and a gentle person. I depended on her for everything. . .I watched her become a strong person, and that had an enormous influence on me.

Rosalynn Carter

Nothing can compare in beauty,
and wonder, and admirableness,
and divinity itself, to the silent work
in obscure dwellings of faithful women
bringing up their children
to honor and virtue and piety.

Henry Ward Beecher

My mother had a slender, small body, but a large heart—a heart so large that everybody's grief and everybody's joys found welcome in it, and hospitable accommodation. The greatest difference which I find between her and the rest of the people whom I have known, is this: those others felt a strong interest in a few things, whereas to the very day of her death, she felt a strong interest in the whole world and everything and everybody in it. In all her life she never knew such a thing as a half-hearted interest in affairs and people, or an interest which drew a line and left out certain affairs and was indifferent to certain people. . . .

Her interest in people and animals was warm, personal, friendly. She was the natural ally and friend of the friendless.

Mark Twain

*A*mother is she who can
take the place of all others,
but whose place
no one else can take.

Cardinal Mermillod

Whatever beauty of poetry
is to be found in my little book
is owing to your interest in and encouragement
of all my efforts from the first to the last;
and if ever I do anything to be proud of,
my greatest happiness will be that I can thank you
for that, as I may do for all the good there is in me;
and I shall be content to write if it gives you pleasure.

Louisa May Alcott to her Mother
December 25, 1854

There is nothing so strong
as the force of love; there is no love so forcible
as the love of an affectionate mother
to her natural child.

Elizabeth Grymeston

I remember my mother's prayers
and they have always followed me.
They have clung to me
all of my life.

Abraham Lincoln

My Mother's Garden

Her heart is like her garden,
Old-fashioned, quaint, and sweet,
With here a wealth of blossoms,
And there a still retreat.
Sweet violets are hiding,
We know as we pass by,
And lilies, pure as angel thoughts,
Are opening somewhere nigh.

Forget-me-nots there linger,
To full perfection brought,
And there bloom purple pansies
In many a tender thought.
There love's won roses blossom,
As from enchanted ground,
And lavish perfume exquisite
The whole glad year around.

Alice E. Allen

Romance fails us—
and so do friendships—
but the relationship of Mother and Child
remains indelible and indestructible—
the strongest bond upon this earth.

Theodor Reik

The mother loves her child most divinely,
not when she surrounds him with comfort
and anticipates his wants, but when
she resolutely holds him
to the highest standards and is content
with nothing less than his best.

—Hamilton Wright Mabie

A mother's love is patient and forgiving
when all others are forsaking,
and it never fails or falters,
even though the heart is breaking.

Helen Steiner Rice

A Mother's Wrinkled Hands

*S*uch beautiful, beautiful hands!
Though heart was weary and sad
Those patient hands kept toiling on
That her children might be glad.
I almost weep when looking back
To childhood's distant day!
I think how these hands rested not
When mine were at their play.

$\mathcal{A}$ mother is the truest friend we have, when trials, heavy and sudden, fall upon us; when adversity takes the place of prosperity; when friends who rejoice with us in our sunshine, desert us when troubles thicken around us, still will she cling to us, and endeavor by her kind precepts and counsels to dissipate the clouds of darkness, and cause peace to return to our hearts. . . . But a mother's love endures through all; in good repute, in bad repute, in the face of the world's condemnation, a mother still loves on, and still hopes that her child may turn from his evil ways, and repent; still she remembers the infant smiles that once filled her bosom with rapture, the merry laugh, the joyful shout of his childhood, the opening promise of his youth; and she can never be brought to think him all unworthy.

Washington Irving

In all my efforts to learn to read, my mother shared fully my ambition and sympathized with me and aided me in every way she could. If I have done anything in life worth attention, I feel sure that I inherited the disposition from my mother.

Booker T. Washington

Everybody knows that a good mother gives her children a feeling of trust and stability. Somehow even her clothes feel different to her children's hands from anybody else's clothes. Only to touch her skirt or her sleeve makes a troubled child feel better.

Katharine Butler Hathaway

A mother is a person who sees
that there are only four pieces of pie
for five persons
and promptly remarks that
she's never cared for pie.

Anonymous

No joy in nature is
so sublimely affecting as
the joy of a mother at
the good fortune of her child.

Jean Paul Richter

Mother is the name for God
in the lips and hearts of children.

William Makepeace Thackeray

❧

There is no influence so powerful
as that of the mother.

Sarah Hale

If you want your children to turn out well,
spend twice as much time with them,
and half as much money.

Abigail Van Buren

*Mommy* herself has told us that she
looked upon us more as her friends than
her daughters. Now that is all very fine, but still,
a friend can't take a mother's place.
I need my mother as an example which I can follow.
I want to be able to respect her.

Anne Frank

There is no friendship,

no love,

like that of

the mother for the child.

Henry Ward Beecher

No matter how lost and soiled
and worn-out wandering sons may be,
mothers can forgive and forget every thing
as they fold them in their fostering arms.

Louisa May Alcott

Dear Mother—

You know that nothing can ever change
what we have always been and always
will be to each other.

Franklin Roosevelt to his Mother
1911

Women Know

*W*omen know
The way to rear up children (to be just)
They have a merry, simple, tender knack
Of tying sashes, fitting babies' shoes,
And stringing pretty words that make no sense,
And kissing full sense into empty words;
Which things are corals to cut life upon
Although such trifles.

Elizabeth Barrett Browning

My mother was an angel upon earth.
She was a minister of blessing to all human beings
within her sphere of action. She had no feelings but
of kindness and beneficence, yet her mind was as
firm as her temper was mild and gentle. She had
been fifty years the delight of my father's heart.

John Quincy Adams

The mother's heart is the child's schoolroom.

Henry Ward Beecher

All mothers are rich
when they love their children.

Maurice Maeterlinck

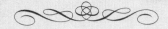

Some are kissing mothers and some
are scolding mothers, but it is love just the same,
and most mothers kiss and scold together.

Pearl S. Buck

So many memories of the past present themselves when one tries to revive in fancy the features of a beloved being, that one views them dimly through these memories, as through tears. These are the tears of imagination. When I try to recall my mother as she was at that time, nothing appears to me but her brown eyes, which always expressed love and goodness; the mole on her neck a little lower down than the spot where the short hairs grow; her white embroidered collar; her cool, soft hand, which petted me so often, and which I so often kissed: but her image as a whole escapes me.

Leo Tolstoy

Our Mother

*A*nd while with care our mother laid
The work aside, her steps she stayed
One moment, seeking to express
Her grateful sense of happiness
For food and shelter, warmth and health,
And love's contentment more than wealth,
With simple wishes not the weak,
Vain prayers which no fulfillment seek,
But such as warm the generous heart.

John Greenleaf Whittier

They always looked back before turning the corner, for their mother was always at the window to nod and smile, and wave her hand at them. Somehow it seemed as if they couldn't have got through the day without that, for whatever their mood might be, the last glimpse of that motherly face was sure to affect them like sunshine.

Louisa May Alcott

A mother has, perhaps, the hardest earthly lot;
and yet no mother worthy of the name
ever gave herself thoroughly for her child
who did not feel that, after all, she reaped
what she had sown.

Henry Ward Beecher

Nothing else will ever make you

as happy or as sad, as proud or as tired,

as motherhood.

Elia Parsons

Youth fades; love droops,
the leaves of friendship fall.
A mother's secret hope
outlives them all.

Oliver Wendell Holmes

*In*life you may have friends fond, dear friends,
but never will you have again
the inexpressible love and gentleness
lavished upon you which
none but a Mother bestows.

Macaulay

Mother

*A*gain your kindly, smiling face I see.
Do I but dream? And do my eyes deceive?
Again you whisper through the years to me,
I feel the pressure of your lips at eve.
I dream once more I sit upon your knee,
And hear sweet counsel that I should not grieve;
My hand in yours at twilight time as we
Talk low, and I your sweet caress receive. . . .

O mother of my childhood's pleasant days!
Still whispering courage and dispelling fears
In daylight hours or quiet moonlight rays,
Are you a dream come from my younger years?
Or do you really walk along the ways,
And know my triumphs, or my inner tears,
That quickly cease when you close by me seem?
Let me sleep on, dear God, if I but dream.

Max Ehrmann

There is only one pretty child in the world,
and every mother has it.

English Proverb

❦

One good mother is worth
a hundred school masters.

George Herbert

If you bungle raising your children,
I don't think whatever else you do well
matters very much.

Jacqueline Kennedy Onassis

The woman who creates and sustains a home,
and under whose hands children grow up
to be strong and pure men and women
is a creator second only to God.

Helen Hunt Jackson

The mother is the most precious possession
of the nation, so precious that society
advances its highest well-being
when it protects the functions
of the mother.

Ellen Kay

The Reading Mother

I had a Mother who read me the things
That wholesome life to the boy heart brings—
Stories that stir with an upward touch,
Oh, that each mother of boys were such!

You may have tangible wealth untold;
Caskets of jewels and coffers of gold.
Richer than I you can never be—
I had a Mother who read to me.

Strickland Gillilan

My mother was the making of me.
She was so true and so sure of me,
I felt that I had someone to live for—
someone I must not disappoint.
The memory of my mother will always
be a blessing to me.

Thomas Edison

To My Mother

They tell us of an Indian tree
Which howso'er the sun and sky
May tempt its boughs to wander free,
And shoot and blossom, wide and high,
Far better love to bend its arms
Downward again to that dear earth
From which the life, that fills and warms
Its grateful being, first had birth.
'Tis thus, though wooed by flattering friends,
And fed with fame (if fame may be),
This heart, my own dear mother, bends,
With love's true instinct, back to thee!

Thomas Moore

My mother's love for me was so great that
I have worked hard to justify it.

Marc Chagall

Mother love is the fuel that enables a
normal human being to do the impossible.

Marion Garretty

Mother of Mine

*M*other in gladness, Mother in sorrow,
Mother today, and Mother tomorrow,
With arms ever open to fold and caress you
O Mother of mine, may God keep you and bless you.

W. Dayton Wedgefarth

Who is it that loves me and will love me
forever with an affection which no chance,
no misery, no crime of mine can do away?
My dear mother, with the truthfulness of
a mother's heart, ministered to all my woes,
outward and inward, and even against hope
kept prophesying good.

Thomas Carlyle

Other things may change us,
but we start and end with the family.

Anthony Brandt

❦

A child without a mother
is like a door without a knob.

Jewish Proverb

 *My* mother was the source
from which I derived
the guiding principles
of my life.

John Wesley

To My Mother

*B*ecause I feel that, in the Heavens above,
The angels, whispering to one another,
Can find, among their burning terms of love,
None so devotional as that of "Mother,"
Therefore by that dear name I long to have called you—
You who are more than mother unto me,
And fill my heart of hearts, where Death installed you,
In setting my Virginia's spirit free.

My mother—my own mother, who died early,
Was but the mother of myself; but you
Are mother to the one I loved so dearly,
And thus are dearer than the mother I knew
By that infinity with which my wife
Was dearer to my soul than its soul-life.

Edgar Allan Poe

Do not, on a rainy day, ask your child
what he feels like doing, because I assure you
that what he feels like doing,
you won't feel like watching.

Fran Lebowitz

*A*suburban mother's role
is to deliver children obstetrically once,
and by car for ever after.

Peter De Vries

There is an enduring tenderness in the love of a mother. It is neither to be chilled by selfishness, nor daunted by danger. She will sacrifice every comfort to his convenience; she will surrender every pleasure to his enjoyment; she will glory in his fame and exalt in his prosperity; and if advisary overtake him, he will be the dearer to her by misfortune; and if disgrace settle upon his name, she will still love and cherish him; and if all the world beside cast him off, she will be all the world to him.

Washington Irving

You don't choose your family,
They are God's gift to you, as you are to them.
Desmond Tutu

❦

My mother was the most beautiful woman
I ever saw. . .all I am I owe to my mother.
George Washington

A mother's heart
is a baby's most beautiful dwelling.
Ed Dussault

❧

Life is the first gift, love is the second,
and understanding the third.
Marge Piercy

73

My Mother's Clothes

*W*hen I was small, my mother's clothes
All seemed so kind to me!
I hid my face amid the folds
As safe as safe could be.

Yes, everything she wore
Received my hopes and fears,
And even the garments of her soul
Contained my smiles and tears.

Then softly I will touch
This dress she used to wear.
The old-time comfort lingers yet,
My smiles and tears are there.

A tenderness abides
Though laid so long away,
And I must kiss their empty folds,
So comfortable are they.

Anna Hempstead Branch

*T*shall never forget my mother, for it was she who planted and nurtured the first seeds of good within me. She opened my heart to the impressions of nature; she awakened my understanding and extended my horizon, and her percepts exerted an everlasting influence upon the course of my life.

Immanuel Kant

The commonest fallacy among women is
that simply having children makes one a mother—
which is as absurd as believing that
having a piano makes one a musician.

Sydney J. Harris

The tie which links mother and child is of such pure and immaculate strength as to be never violated, except by those feelings that are withered by vitiated society. Holy, simple, and beautiful in its construction, it is the emblem of all we can imagine of fidelity and truth. In all our trials, amid all our afflictions, she is still by our side; if we sin, she reproves more in sorrow than in anger; nor can she tear us from her bosom, nor forget we are her child.

Washington Irving

A Valentine to My Mother

My blessed Mother dozing in her chair
On Christmas Day seemed an embodied Love,
A comfortable Love with soft brown hair
Softened and silvered to a tint of dove;
A better sort of Venus with an air
Angelical from thoughts that dwell above;
A wiser Pallas in whose body fair
Enshrined a blessed soul looks out thereof.

Winter brought holly then; now Spring has brought
Paler and frailer snowdrops shivering;
And I have brought a simple humble thought—
I her dutious Valentine—
A lifelong thought which drills this song I sing,
A lifelong love to this dear saint of mine.

Christina G. Rossetti

Beautiful as seemed mamma's face, it became incomparably more lovely when she smiled, and seemed to enliven everything about her. If in life's trying moments I could catch but a glimpse of that smile, I should not know what grief is. It seems to me that what is called beauty of face consists in the smile alone: if the smile adds charm to the face, then the face is very fine; if it does not alter the countenance, then the latter is ordinary; if it spoils, then it is bad.

Leo Tolstoy

Her Mother

*O*h, if I could only make you see
The clear blue eyes, the tender smile,
The sovereign sweetness, the gentle grace,
The woman's soul, the angel's face
That are beaming on me all the while,
I need not speak these foolish words:
Yet one word tells you all I would say,—
She is my mother: you will agree
That all the rest may be thrown away.
Alice Cary

A mother holds her children's hands for a while,
their hearts forever.

Anonymous

The imprint of the mother remains forever on
the life of the child.

Anonymous

Mothers are the most unselfish, the most responsible people in the world.
Bernard Baruch

Childhood is like a mirror, which reflects in after life the images first presented to it.
Samuel Smiles

Who is it that loves me and will love me forever with an affection that no chance, no misery, no crime of mine can do away?

It is you, my mother.

Thomas Carlyle

Mother

You painted no Madonnas on chapel walls in Rome;
But, with a touch diviner, upon the walls of home.

You wrote no lofty poems with rare poetic art;
But with a finer vision, you put poems in my heart.

You carved no shapeless marble to symmetry divine;
But, with a nobler genius, you shaped this soul of mine.

You built no great cathedrals, the centuries applaud;
But, with a grace exquisite, your heart was
house of God.

Had I the gift of Raphael, or Michael Angelo,
Oh, what a rare Madonna my mother's life
would show.

Thomas W. Fessenden

Of all the rights of women, the greatest is
to be a mother.
Lin Yutang

A kiss from my mother made me a painter.
Benjamine West

Mothers are made of tenderness,
and sweet sleep blesses the child
who lies therein.

Victor Hugo

Mother

For such as you, I do believe,
Spirits their softest carpets weave,
And spread them out with gracious hand
Wherever you walk, wherever you stand.

For such as you, of scent and dew
Spirits their rarest nectar brew,

And where you sit and where you sup
Pour beauty's elixir in your cup.

For all day long, like other folk,
You bear the burden, wear the yoke,
And yet when I look in to your eyes at eve
You are lovelier than ever, I do believe.

Herman Hagedorn

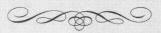

Every mother is like Moses. She does not enter the promised land. She prepares a world she will not see.

Pope Paul VI

❧

Many make the household but only one the home.

James Russell Lowell

There is no love like the good old love—the love that mother gave us.

Eugene Field

❦

A mother's children are like ideas; none are as wonderful as her own.

Chinese Proverb

Cleaning your house while
your kids are still growing
is like shoveling the walk
before it stops snowing.

Phyllis Diller

Any mother could perform
the jobs of several
air traffic controllers with ease.

Lisa Alther

Sonnets Are Full of Love,
And This My Tome

*S*onnets are full of love, and this my tome
Has many sonnets: so here now shall be
One sonnet more, a love sonnet, from me
To her whose heart is my heart's quiet home,
To my first Love, my Mother, on whose knee
I learnt love-lore that is not troublesome;

Whose service is my special dignity,
And she my loadstar while I go and come.
And so because you love me, and because
I love you, Mother, I have woven a wreath
Of rhymes wherewith to crown your honored name:
In you not fourscore years can dim the flame
Of love, whose blessed glow transcends the laws
Of time and change and mortal life and death.

Christina Rossetti

All that I am, or hope to be,
I owe to my angel mother.
Abraham Lincoln

What the mother sings to the cradle goes
all the way down to the coffin.
Henry Ward Beecher

100

Rejecting things because they are
old-fashioned would rule out
the sun and the moon—
and a mother's love.

Anonymous

Mother

*A*s long ago we carried to your knees
The tales and treasures of eventful days,
Knowing no deed too humble for your praise,
Nor any gift too trivial to please,
So still we bring with older smiles and tears,
What gifts we may to claim the old, dear right;
Your faith beyond the silence and the night;
Your love still close and watching through the years.

Anonymous

102

Mother means selfless devotion, limitless sacrifice, and love that passes understanding.

Anonymous

⬥⬥⬥

A family unit is composed not only of children, but of fathers, mothers, an occasional animal and at times, the common cold.

Ogden Nash

Mother love is that divine gift which comforts, purifies, and strengthens all who seek it.

Louisa May Alcott

A hundred men may make an encampment, but it takes a woman to make a home.

Chinese Proverb

The finest inheritance you can give
to a child is to allow it to make its own way,
completely on its own feet.
Isadora Duncan

was between three and four years of age when our mother died, and my own personal recollections of her are therefore but few. But the deep interest and veneration that she inspired in all who knew her was such that, during my childhood, I was constantly hearing her spoken of, and, from one friend or another, some incident or anecdote of her life was constantly being impressed on me. Mother was one of those strong, restful, yet widely sympathetic natures, in whom all around seemed to find comfort and repose. Although mother's bodily presence disappeared from our circle, I think that her memory and example had more influence in molding her family, in deterring from evil and exciting to good, than the living presence of many mothers. It was a memory that met us everywhere, for every person in town, from the highest to the lowest, seemed to have been so impressed by her character and life that they constantly reflected some portion of it back on us.

Harriet Beecher Stowe

I think my life began with waking up
and loving my mother's face.
George Eliot

❧

There is a harmony and beauty in the life of
mother and son that brims the
mind's cup of satisfaction.
Christopher Morley

When we see great men and women,
we give credit to their mothers.
Charlotte Perkins Gilman

❦

The best things you can give children,
next to good habits, are good memories.
Sydney J. Harris

There are only two things a child will
share willingly—communicable diseases
and his mother's age.

Benjamin Spock

There was never a child so lovely

but his mother was glad

to get him asleep.

Ralph Waldo Emerson

My Trust

A picture memory brings to me:
I look across the years and see
Myself beside my mother's knee.
I feel her gentle hand restrain
My selfish moods, and know again
A child's blind sense of wrong and pain.
But wiser now, a man grey grown,
My childhood's needs are better known,
My mother's chastening love I own.

John Greenleaf Whittier

A mother is a parent who remains
sane only because she never knows
what her three-year-old is going to do next.

Evan Esar

Child and Mother

*O*Mother-My Love, if you'll give me your hand
And go where I ask you to wander,
I will lead you away to a beautiful land—
The dreamland that's waiting out yonder.
We'll walk in the sweet posie gardens out there,
Where moonlight and starlight are streaming,
And the flowers and the birds are filling the air
With the fragrance and music of dreaming.

Eugene Field

*Every* mother of more than one
child has a secret favorite,
so secret that she might go through
her whole life and never admit to herself
which one it was.

Gail Godwin

When you are a mother, you are never really alone in your thoughts.
You are connected to your child and to all those who touch your lives.

Sophia Loren

Mother, I love you so.

Said the child, I love you more than I know.

She laid her head on her mother's arm,

And the love between them kept them warm.

Stevie Smith

Home Is Where There's One To Love Us

*H*ome is not merely four square walls,
Though with pictures hung and gilded;
Home is were Affection calls,
Filled with shrines the Heart hath builded!
Home!—go watch the faithful dove,
Sailing `neath the heaven above us;
Home is where there's one to love!
Home is where there's one to love us!

Home's not merely roof and room—
It needs something to endear it;
Home is where the heart can bloom,
Where there's some kind lip to cheer it!
What is home with none to meet,
None to welcome,none to greet us?
Home is sweet—and only sweet—
Where there's one we love to meet us!

Charles Swain

Most of all the other beautiful things in life
come by twos and threes, by dozens and
hundreds. Plenty of roses, stars, sunsets,
rainbows, brothers and sisters, aunts and cousins,
but only one mother in the whole world.

Kate Douglas Wiggin

Mother

As long ago we carried to your knees
The tales and treasures of eventful days,
Knowing no deed too humble for your praise,
Nor any gift too trivial to please,
So still we bring with older smiles and tears,
What gifts we may to claim the old, dear right;
Your faith beyond the silence and the night;
Your love still close and watching through the years.

Anonymous

121

Other Penbrooke Books You Will Enjoy:

Love Letters To Remember (ISBN # 1-889116-02-5)

Letters to Mother (ISBN # 1-889116-00-9)

Joy of Christmas (ISBN # 1-889116-06-8)

Sister of Mine (ISBN # 1-889116-08-4)

Everlasting Friendship (ISBN # 1-889116-04-1)

Significant Acts of Kindness (ISBN # 1-889116-01-7)

A Timeless Gift of Love (ISBN # 1-889116-05-X)

A Tribute to Dad (ISBN # 1-889116-13-0)

The Little Book of Happies (ISBN # 1-889116-03-3)

My False Teeth Fit Fine, But I Sure Miss My Mind (ISBN # 1-889116-07-6)

To order additional copies of this book, or any of our other books,
call toll-free 1-888-493-2665

PENBROOKE
PUBLISHING
P. O. Box 700566
Tulsa, OK 74170